The Path To Home Ownership

Your Path Is Just A Few

Short Steps Away!

Written By

Louis Brown

Published by *Nomad CEO Publishing*

ISBN-13:978-1503076341

ISBN-10:1503076342

Legal Disclaimer

Disclaimer and Terms of Use: The Author and Publisher have strived to be as accurate and complete as possible in the creation of this book, notwithstanding the fact that they do not warrant or represent at any time that the contents within are accurate due to the rapidly changing nature of the Internet. While all attempts have been made to verify information provided in this publication, the Author and Publisher assume no responsibility for errors, omissions, or contrary interpretation of the subject matter herein. Any perceived slights of specific persons, peoples, or organizations are unintentional. In practical advice books, like anything else in life, there are no guarantees of income made. Readers are cautioned to rely on their own judgment about their individual circumstances to act accordingly. This book is not intended for use as a source of legal, business, accounting or financial advice. All readers are advised to seek services of competent professionals in the legal, business, accounting, and finance fields.

Table of Contents

Introduction

Still dreaming of owning your own home, but afraid you won't qualify? Wondering how to buy a house with non-traditional methods?

Well, you're not alone.

Currently over 100 MILLION families and individuals in America do not own a home of their own. This is the lowest ownership rate in over 70 years. The reason is that 80% of Americans today cannot qualify for a traditional bank loan. This fact presents a real barrier to advancing the ideals of owning a slice of the American Dream.

Path To Home Ownership® was designed to educate, then connect individuals and families who are looking to someday own a home with experienced and qualified Certified Affordable Housing Providers® (CAHPs) who want to do good by providing affordable housing to the public. If you are looking to rent or Rent to Own, but one day dream of owning your own home, look no further. Welcome to your personal Path to Home Ownership™.

Many perceive that "Affordable Housing" is about providing low cost or low quality housing for the poor. This is simply not true.

"Affordable Housing Payments" might be a better description of how the Path to Home Ownership® program works. We provide housing with monthly payments of equal to or less than one-third of a family's combined monthly gross income. Therefore, "Affordable Housing" is not just a description of the housing that qualifies, but also a description of what a person or family can afford.

We only offer a person or family housing they can sustain... based on their current income. Our Certified Affordable Housing Providers® (CAHP's) are trained to look at your income and other financial obligations to determine what monthly price range and price point you can qualify for. We then work with you to help you find the perfect home for your family, one you can eventually own, inside of your budget.

The first step in the process is to obtain your credit report. While you may have already obtained a credit report, this is a special kind. It's what credit lenders and banks use to qualify you for a home.

You simply pay a fee based on whether you are an individual or a married couple to your local CAHP (pronounced CAP). They either provide you the access information or enter it for you to obtain a credit analysis. This gives your CAHP guidance on how best to serve you. The analysis provider will give an indication of how quickly they believe you will be able to attain qualifying for a bank loan.

For some people, that could be as short as 30 days. For others, it could take up to two years. For those who have challenges on their credit report, they can suggest solutions for that.

That could include a recommendation to join a nationally recognized credit repair program. They may also suggest Secured credit cards or other methods to increase your credit score to be able to obtain a bank loan.

In the meantime, your local CAHP will begin looking for a home to match your set of circumstances, as will be explained.

What types of Affordable Housing programs does PTHO offer?

Are you wondering where to find Rent to Own homes? Do you want to get into your own home in less time? CAHPs participating in the PTHO program offer Rent, Rent to Own (Lease with Option to Buy), Owner Financing (Agreement for Deed), and Cash Sale (New Bank Loan) options (where not restricted by state law). Even a renter is given a plan to follow so that eventually owning a home is possible. You are placed in our membership program starting at the level you can afford now, based on your initial investment. Then you are given options and opportunities to boost to the next membership level until you can eventually buy the home.

So kick back and read on to find out how you, too, can become a home owner, stop lining the pockets of your landlord with your hard earned money, and put yourself and your family in a position to *Never Pay Rent Again*!

Lou Brown

Chapter 1

Doing Good While Doing Well

"If it is to be - it is up to me!"

Our business inspires me!

That's a rare statement for a lot of business owners to make. But for me, it is absolutely true. I think back to when I was a kid. There are two distinct things I remember from my childhood: money was tough, and I really had no one to fall back on.

My mom had made some bad decisions about life partners, and it ended up being just her and me against the world. Now this was back in the day when there were not a lot of government programs to help out. I'm not sure, but I don't think it would've mattered. My mother was proud, and did not really want or seek help from others.

You see, my mom was from Scotland. She came over as a war bride, and all of her family was in Scotland. We were estranged from my father, and hence, his entire family. So that just left us.

I know what it's like to have no money. I know what it's like to hide out from the rent man. My mom would say "shhh, don't say anything... I'll have the money by this weekend." She just didn't want to face anyone and have to say that.

Now I didn't know it then, but the universe was starting it's alignment with my journey in life.

I never will forget the one time we went to see some of her friends. I called them 'aunts' and 'uncles,' as I had none. I was about eight years old and Aunt Mabel told me a story. She said they had just bought the duplex they lived in. She told me they went to the bank, got a loan, and that the people on the other side were paying enough money in rent the cover the mortgage. What did she just say?? Even at that age I realized that what she said was that they were living there for free!!

Can you imagine how that captured my imagination? Now of course, I didn't know anything about finances or money or how other people even lived. The one thing I did know was - *we* didn't have the money for rent sometimes, and *she* didn't have to pay any.

That's probably where I got the first insight that there really are parallel universes out there. Some people struggle with money, and others don't. Some people put forth the effort to think and educate themselves and uncover truths that are unknown to those who do not.

Wow! So all I have to do is remember that there are people fortunate enough to apply themselves and in return, get pieces of information that allow them to break the money code.

The Money Code

The money code is quite fascinating. I am definitely a student of it. Some people work their entire lives and end up with very little to show for it, while others seem to effortlessly move through life and always have plenty of money to spend. So, what's the difference?

I recall that my mother (God rest her soul) was one of the ones who did not take the time nor gain the tools to master money -Money mastered her. I did not like the process, and saw how high interest on borrowed money could eat a fortune in a hurry.

So I watched and studied the processes involved. We visited Aunt Mabel and she told us she had bought the duplex next door and that the people on that side were paying enough in rent to cover the mortgage, with enough left over to go into their pockets. I watched their lifestyle change: a new Cadillac every other year, nice furniture, trips, and cruises. And they ate out at the steakhouse almost every night!

They just kept buying real estate. One day Aunt Mabel called me and asked me to help her move. They had just bought a brand-new house. It was a two-story, all brick home, in a brand-new subdivision, on a corner lot. Far more house than she, Uncle George, and their two Chihuahuas needed.

"How did you do this, Mabel?" was my question. She said two words that changed my life: **Accumulate Property.**

Now, this parallel universe continued. When I was about 12 years old, my mother heard about a program that would allow us to buy a home. It was a modest three-bedroom home. It was very exciting and things looked positive. Then after form after form were completed and time passed, we were told that she did not qualify.

This devastated her. She didn't say much, but I could tell it really took the wind out of her sails. It was something that she wanted for me. She wanted me out of those apartments – those terrible apartments – and get me into something better, more room, a better location and in turn, a better life.

That was not to be. It affected her so badly that she never tried again.

The Path To Home Ownership

Several years later when I was about 18 years, old Aunt Mabel said to me "hey, you need to buy a house." I said "yeah, that would be nice, Aunt Mabel, but you've bought all your property by qualifying for loans. I can't qualify my way out of a paper bag."

She laughed and said I needed to meet her friend 'Realtor Sue.' One phone call and realtor Sue was anxious to show me some property. You see, I had worked very hard during my teenage years. I had first started a paper route when I was 11 years old (actually, I was not supposed to start till 12, but I fibbed a bit.) I wanted to get ahead, and I figured this was a chance.

Every chance I got I saved up money and worked after school jobs and did other things to make things work. I knew one thing – I wanted a better life for myself and my mom.

It didn't take long until realtor Sue found a house that I liked. Turns out, I could buy this house differently than Aunt Mabel did.

Again, I discovered a parallel universe: those who go to banks and qualify for loans and buy property, versus those who buy property a different way.

And the second way made all the difference.

Essentially.... it's to use the seller as the bank.

I ended up buying my first property at the age of 19, without even going to a bank or qualifying for a loan. That was a real eye-opener!

My mother became my first tenant, paying me $100 per month (along with washing some clothes and cooking some meals. ☺) It was a good deal for me because it helped make ends meet, but it was also a good deal for her. Our rent was about $600 per month, and I told her to take $500 per month and put it towards her debt. Within a year and a half she was debt-free for the rest of her life. That was a new experience for her.

I got to see first-hand that if my mother had discovered this other universe when I was 12 years old, then I would not have spent my teenage years in an apartment.

Knowledge is power. In fact, I teach that 'Knowledge is Power *and Money*.'

As time passed, I was transferred by the company I worked for from Charlotte, North Carolina to Atlanta, Georgia. Why not? My mom was all set and the company offered to pay my closing costs if I would sell my house and buy a new one down there. So I did, and in the process I was surprised to see that in less than two years my property had gone up by 37%!

In Atlanta I again decided not to qualify for a loan, even though I could have. I told the agent to find me a house where the seller would be the bank.

Once again it happened, and to this day I have ***never*** qualified for a loan from a bank for a single-family or small multifamily property. There was - and is - no reason to. Why would I?

I also started to realize that if I offered my real estate the same way to the people who wanted to live there, then I could help change their lives as well. Why should they be relegated to being renters for the rest of their lives?

I could become the bank for them as the seller, and give them what I would eventually call "The Path to Home Ownership.'®

Inspiration

I started this story with "Our Business Inspires Me!" Likely now you can understand why I think so. Imagine working with a couple or a family and showing them that there is another way.

Imagine giving them a leg up in life and an opportunity that no one else has given them. Imagine working with them to help them improve their credit to the point that they can get a new loan. Or just be the bank for them and give them pride of ownership and the opportunity of possibility.

I have so many stories of people we have helped. One was a 63 year old gentleman who had never owned a home in his name in his life. He started out with our *Work for Equity Program* and did all the repairs to the home with the help of his family and friends. We credited that work towards his down payment. This allowed him the opportunity to work with a credit repair program and get his credit cleaned up so that he could get a new bank loan.

Another success story was a nurse. She loved the idea of our *Work for Equity Program* and even though she didn't have a lot of experience, she went to training sessions at the local builder supply store and learned how to do her own tile and sheet rock work. She transformed her home and made it look absolutely beautiful. We became the bank for her, and have been her bank for over five years now.

We also have a couple in the Chattanooga, Tennessee area that lived in a mobile home on her father's land for over 20 years. We had a beautiful home available on 5 acres of land, and have become the bank for these nice people for the past four years.

The stories are endless, and the challenges that human beings face are much more intense than I had to face.

People who are selling their homes are drawn to our program. They see that the home that they have enjoyed and raised their children in can be passed along through our process to a deserving family who will be raising their family there, while helping the community, as well.

Not only are sellers attracted to our program because they can help a deserving family, but we have also found that individuals who have retirement accounts such as IRAs or 401(k)'s and personal funds love to lend to our CAHP's because they see that their money is being used to help people, while also earning a nice return as well.

This is the essence of what Certified Affordable Housing Providers do:

1) They find and assist families and individuals to find the right home that they desire that is also affordable.
2) Then they seek out families and individuals who have a home but want to move (for whatever reason) and assist them in a quick and fair sale of their home to the CAHP. Often this is facilitated by the seller acting as the bank for a short period of time.

3) In some instances when homes can be bought from HUD or Banks and cash is needed for the purchase, then individuals and families with IRAs, 401(k)'s, and personal funds can be used and those lenders can earn much higher than the paltry sum the bank or stock market is paying them for their funds.

CAHP's invest in their education and go through extensive training, while also being provided essential tools and forms to effectively help everyone participating in the process and make a living for themselves and their family.

So as you can see, everyone wins: the Buyer or renter gets the home of their needs, the Seller gets their property sold quick and easy at a fair price, and Private Lenders get to deploy their funds at higher rates than the bank pays, with less risk than the stick (I mean stock) market.

Doing Good While Doing Well® is the essence of what a CAHP is.

Once you are finished reading this book, please do pass it on to others who may not even realize that they have the possibility of becoming a homeowner. You can really help someone else down life's road, just as your local CAHP is showing you.

If you find that you are interested in becoming a Certified Affordable Housing Provider® then be sure to visit **CertifiedAffordableHousingProvider.com** or call **1-800-578-8580** and say that you read about it in this book. Be ready to tell them who your local CAHP is, as they will ask.

Chapter 2

Taking the Fear Out of Home Buying

For many years I have worked with hundreds of individuals and families looking to purchase their first home. But over and over again I still hear the same questions being asked: "Am I ready for this commitment?" or "Don't you think I'm too young to buy?" or "What happens if I lose my job?" or "Can I really afford to buy a house? Shouldn't I just keep renting?"

Yes, I will agree that buying a home, especially your first home, can be a daunting experience, and scary as hell! But because I have been able to answer these questions for many years, I am qualified to say that you have to get past these excuses. Get past the negativity. Buying a home can be an easy process, especially when you have the right person steering you on the right path.

Remember what it was like the first time you had your own apartment? When you first walked in the door and thought to yourself "this is all mine." Can you still feel the exhilaration that you felt then? Well, multiply that 100 times when you walk in the front door to a home that you now ***own.*** It is yours. Not a landlord's. You are not paying someone for the privilege of living in their property. Even though you are paying a mortgage, which can be equated to your monthly rental, you are gaining equity. Instead of making a payment that goes nowhere, you are now investing in your future. You now have the option of selling it in a few years for a profit, or maybe even renting it out, which will put more money in your pocket every month. And think about the tax break you will get every year!

I believe that there is no better feeling than when you say 'good bye' to your landlord. Imagine waking up in the morning excited to be able to paint the walls a color that you like, or replacing the dripping faucets in the bathroom, or building that herb garden that you so desperately wanted, and nobody can tell you "no you can't." That feeling is absolutely priceless.

Instead of seeing that $1,000 a month fly out the window, (and making the landlord richer) it is now working for you. It is building equity. And what exactly is equity? It is the difference between the market value of your home and what you owe on it. Let me explain:

Let's say that you are purchasing a home for $200,000. You put $10,000 (or 5%) down. The amount that you provided, $10,000, is the equity in your home. Every month that you make a payment towards that loan the principal (loan amount) reduces, while the value of your home (equity) goes up.

And wouldn't it be great to be able to receive a refund at tax time instead of always paying out because you rent? Deductions are the key, and believe it or not, there are still deductions that you can take:

- Mortgage Interest
- Moving Costs
- Real Estate Taxes
- Points
- Home Improvements
- Private Mortgage Insurance Premiums
- Penalty-free IRA payouts for first-time buyers
- Home equity loans

Having these additional deductions could mean thousands of dollars in tax savings for you each and every year. In addition, if you decide to sell your home after living in it for two out of five years, the first $25,000 of profit is tax free. Now if you are married, the profit doubles to $50,000. Isn't it nice to have such a great savings plan?

Not convinced yet that buying a home is the right thing to do? Let me help you by answering a few of the questions and concerns that I have gotten over the years:

1. **"I just can't afford to buy right now"**
   The reality is that you might not be able to afford a $350,000 house right now, but you might be able to afford a $150,000 house today.
2. **"What if I lose my job?"**
   Regardless if you are renting or owning, you still need to find a way to support yourself and your family. If you are really that worried, then take the time to learn about disability, unemployment and mortgage insurance coverage.
3. **"I'm afraid to buy in this unstable economy"**
   Have you heard of a "buyer's market?" This is where there are more houses for sale than buyers. Because of this, sellers tend to be a little more flexible with pricing and terms. They just want to get their house sold.
4. **"I don't have enough down payment"**
   Usually this means that you don't have enough down payment for the $350,000, but you have more than enough for the $150,000. Plus, there are many no-money down programs available, which we will get to shortly.
5. **"I'm not sure what I should buy"**
   You're not alone. First and foremost, *trust your gut.* If you don't like the upkeep of a yard, go for a condo. If you like the freedom that a detached home gives you, buy a single family. If you don't

like stairs, buy a ranch. Just remember to keep an open mind when you go house hunting. You never know what will strike your fancy.

6. **"It's a lot of responsibility"**
   So is learning to drive. So is paying your bills on time. But you learned how to do those. Relax. It's not brain surgery!
7. **"I don't know anything about maintenance or home repairs!"**
   Who really does when they first start out? I didn't. But there are classes at Home Depot, Books, DVD's, HGTV Shows, the Internet, and YouTube. Get the picture?

Keep in mind that very few people are calm, cool and collected when they are buying their first home. But it's very easy to reduce your fears when you are prepared with all the tools, knowledge and resources. Plus, having the support of a great real estate member will make your hunt for the perfect home a lot easier.

On The Other Hand....

Renting might still be your best option ***IF***:

- **Your credit needs a lot of work.** Having two of three credit scores above 640 is a necessary requirement in this new real estate market. If you are not there yet, then you need to get the help of a professional to assist you. We have those resources for you. We found the best and they have helped others attain success with our Path To Home Ownership® (PTHO). They can help you, too.

- **You are moving cross-country within months.** If your ideal dream of living the good life is hauling your entire life back and forth cross country several times a year, then owning a home may hold you back from your dream life.
- **Your income will be dramatically decreased.** However, you may still be able to afford a smaller home or condo, but you should wait until your new level of income is determined.
- **Owning a home costs you three times what rents costs in your area.** There are some parts of the country where you really have to be a millionaire to buy a home. In this case you have two choices: continue to make the rich even richer by paying rent, or buy in a different town or neighborhood.
- **You honestly do not have two nickels to rub together.** There are always costs to be paid out of pocket for the appraisal, home inspection, etc. For example, when you moved into your apartment you may have needed first, last and one month's security deposit. Well, buying a house is an even bigger decision than renting an apartment, so you also need

to have *at least* two to three months of mortgage payments.

- **You need to have options.** If you spend half the year in Costa Rica and the other half in France, then you only need a hotel room when you are in town to repack for the next move. You most likely do not need a 2,500 square foot raised ranch in Tampa, Florida.

Chapter 3

Does Buying A House "The Old Fashioned Way" Still Work Today?

Everyone turned to stare at Dave and Debra as if they just stepped off an alien spaceship. Then her dad finally spoke up: "I don't understand why you would spend month after month driving through neighborhood after neighborhood, sign a contract on this house, spend over $1,000 for an inspection and appraisal, and now try to figure out what's happening? And how could you buy a home for $275,000 when your budget is only $225,000?"

They both seemed to have lost their wills to speak, but finally Dave gathered his courage to let their families know the reason why he and Debra thought that finally closing on their new house would be the easiest part of the house buying process. After all, they just "knew" that everything would work itself out. "And besides," Debra said, "other people in my office bought homes and everything worked out for them. And," she added defensively, "after we realized how little we knew about what we were doing, we went online and read all about real estate."

"So," Debra's dad said, "let me understand this. You invested a lot of energy, money and time into buying this house without knowing the answers to some of the major questions? Do you know if you qualify for any down payment programs? What happens if the appraisal comes in way low? Are you sure the sellers didn't rip you off or 'forget' to disclose anything? Seriously. Did you actually think that 'everything would work out fine' because someone in your office did it, too?"

Hang on. Before you close and put this book down, I know that you are probably thinking that you would never do anything like this. But let me tell you this: over the years I have seen and heard this exact same scenario played out again and again and again. However, in Dave and Debra's defense, they aren't the only ones to blame for this disturbing situation. Truth be told, the "traditional" way that most people are taught to buy a home creates this exact situation for many would-be homebuyers.

Dave and Debra's process all began when they both agreed that they needed to be grown-ups by having their own house. Although Debra wanted to buy before they got married, Dave suggested they wait and use the money that they receive from their guests to add to their down payment. Let's try and see exactly where this process started to unravel:

1) They looked at ads in newspapers, on-line, and attended open houses to see exactly what was out there.
2) At one of the open houses they found and hired a real estate agent who gave them a "good vibe."
3) They used their real estate agent's lender to get pre-approved for a mortgage of $225,000 with five percent down.
4) They asked the mortgage lender about down payment assistance programs. (He said he would get back to them once they found a potential house.)
5) After Dave and Debra's beautiful wedding they hurried to their honeymoon suite to find out they received $2,500 in monetary gifts.
6) After combining the $2,500 with their saving of $5,000, they were still short of their $11,250 that they required as a down payment.
7) Not finding anything they liked in their price range, they asked the loan officer to raise their loan from $225,000 to $250,000. Done!
8) They submitted an offer of $275,000 for a house listed at $295,000. Their offer was

accepted, with the seller contributing $5,000 towards closing costs.

9) After advising their loan officer of their good news they once again asked about down payment programs. Even though the loan officer had not yet found a down payment program, he was hopeful. Nevertheless, they were advised that they had to proceed with the home inspection and appraisal because the down payment assistance program required those for the approval.
10) Several weeks later their loan officer still had not found a down payment program. Afraid that they might lose their dream home, along with their earnest money, Dave and Debra have decided to dip into their 401K's and borrow money from their families.

Were you able to see where Dave and Debra made their crucial mistake? If not, don't worry. They actually made several critical errors:

Mistake #1: Dave and Debra started out by seeing what was "out there." Where's the sense in driving yourself into a buying frenzy before you actually have the down payment or know if you can even qualify or afford the house you are interested in?

Mistake #2: They hired the real estate agent who was representing the seller! Do you see the problem with this? Let me give you an example: What if your lawyer was also representing the person who was pressing charges against you? Who would the lawyer actually be working for?

Mistake #3: They went way outside of their maximum price range without knowing how they would come up with the down payment, or seriously considering whether or not they could actually afford it.

Over the years I have seen and heard numerous real estate experts give advice to first-timer home buyers. While some of their advice is constructive, the way in which they advise buyers does not always apply. For example, what if Dave and Debra had decided to stop looking at houses until their loan officer found them a down payment program? Their real estate agent might have been upset and they would have been forced to wait a little longer for their new home, but it's definitely better to wait a little longer than losing your deposit, being stressed out and facing the awkwardness of having to borrow money from family.

So here are my top reasons to scratch buying a home the "old-fashioned" way:

1. **You become oblivious to the true steps of the home buying process.**
   When you are purchasing your first home, you don't have a reference point to compare things to. If you just "go with the flow," you won't know what to expect next. There needs to be a step-by-step guide during the whole home buying process.
2. **It can give you outdated, inappropriate or inaccurate information.**
   Buying a home in Atlanta, Georgia is not the same as buying a house in Woodland, Alabama. So use the internet to find current information about the area.
3. **People think that loan officers and real estate agents take the time to educate you on every step of the process.**
   Unfortunately, there are many realtors who only want to make a fast buck. They don't feel the need to educate their clients, so it's up to you to do your due diligence. But if you do have questions, ask!
4. **There's the assumption that you actually know how to negotiate with your real estate agent,**

home inspector, appraiser, loan officer, insurance agent, etc.
Do you know how to talk to your loan officer about interest rates, points and miscellaneous fees? Do you feel comfortable asking your real estate agent about commission fees? You need to learn what to ask so you don't lose thousands of dollars that you really can't afford to lose.

5. **It doesn't take into account mortgage programs that might be available in your area.**
   Based on certain criteria, every city, town and state offers different mortgage programs. Find out what you can qualify for in your area.
6. **Not everyone has ten, twenty, or fifty thousand dollars just lying around the house.**
   I just love it when some real estate experts casually state "well, you only need twenty percent down." Depending on the area and the price of the home, twenty percent could be ten, twenty or fifty thousand dollars! For the average working Joe, it could take ten years or more to save up that kind of money. But on the other hand, you could be paying that much in rent!

It's necessary to have answers to your questions way before you sign legally binding contracts. Why would you sign forms and documents and make agreements before you know exactly what to expect next? You need a comprehensive resource specialized for your area in order to choose the perfect house, in the ideal neighborhood, at a bargain price.

The one and only way you should make the biggest financial decision of your life is by being armed with *local* real estate knowledge, and a team of honest, *expert* local real estate professionals. Note the emphasis on *local* and *expert*. I cannot stress how many horror stories I have heard from smart homebuyers who mistakenly placed their faith in a voice on the other end of the phone. That voice could be two thousand miles away and never to be heard from if there are any problems.

Another problem I see is that homebuyers might tend to entrust one of their most important financial decisions to a "newbie" right out of real estate school because they feel they know the current ins-and-outs of real estate. Don't get me wrong. I deeply believe in supporting professionals who are just starting out in their profession, but I also believe in having experienced and expert advice when it comes to my money. Don't you?

Your local Certified Affordable Housing Provider® is trained to help you avoid the many mistakes and pitfalls that homeowners make. By beginning with your tri-merge (All three credit agencies Information merged into one report) credit analysis they make sure that you do not commit to more home then you can afford, or a higher payment then you can handle.

Your local CAHP is also aware of local and national down payment and repair assistance programs. These programs vary and come and go based on time frames and funding availability. Often they require a certain credit score and can only be provided at the time of actual deed transfer to the buyer. Your local CAHP will make you aware of local programs you may be able to qualify for after obtaining your credit analysis.

Chapter 4

Is There Such A Thing As Finding That Perfect House?

There are more than enough housing options to suit every homebuyer, regardless of the real estate market. For example, for the last several years, if you were looking for a townhouse or condo you could pretty much find the pick of the litter for less than $300,000 in Miami Beach. By the same token, if you were searching for a nice single family home to start a family, you would do well to consider Marietta, Georgia, where you can find a home for an average sales price of under $150,000. However, the real issue facing most first-time homebuyers is how to find the perfect home for their needs, wants and future plans, all with a price tag that they can afford.

The first step in finding your dream home does not start with spending a dozen weekend's running back and forth to open houses. The first step you need to take in order to find your dream house is to focus on yourself. When I say yourself, this also includes your significant other, children, extended family (pets) and any other important decision makers who will be impacted by the decision. This process starts at your current apartment while sitting down watching television or over dinner. In this chapter I will cover a multitude of variables that you may or may not have considered when examining yourself. I'm sure there will be some that may apply to you that I have not listed. Therefore, use what I provide as an outline in regards to determining your needs. However, you will need to follow my system to come to a decision without jeopardizing your down payment money.

One of the major challenges facing most homebuyers is that as a renter you were only required to look twelve months into your housing future because you were most likely just signing a twelve-month lease on an apartment. However, it is a whole new ballgame when it comes to buying a home. At a minimum you must think at least seven to ten years into the future, and this also means considering many additional factors such as your lifestyle, family plans for the future, convenience to job and your neighborhood, just to name a few.

Rediscovering You and Your Family

The first step on the path of finding your dream home is knowing exactly what you personally want to do with your new home. It is imperative that you hone in on exactly what your lifestyle needs and wants are. For example:

- **Are you planning on living alone, with your spouse or small family?** Consider the fact that life sometimes sends us unintended expansion projects (pregnancy, parent's needs) to test our flexibility. An extra bedroom would be really valuable.
- **What lifestyle choices do you need to stick to?** By the time you are old enough to buy a home, there are some things you just do not want to give up: closeness to downtown area, blocks from park, good schools, nearness to family, etc. Take this into consideration when looking at homes.
- **What is a day or night like at home for you?** Are you the kind of person who would rather curl up and read a book all day in a quiet place in your home, or do you prefer the loud thumping bass of techno music? Are you handy with home repairs, or do you just run for the phone book as fast as you can anytime there is a problem?
- **What are your plans for the home?** Know your goals. You may want to run your own home-based business, so you may need an extra bedroom or home office, or maybe you are looking for a nice little garden that you've always dreamed of.

House Features

When it comes to the tangible elements of your ideal home you will want to start with some of the good and bad elements of the apartment or house you are living in currently. Maybe you love the hardwood floors in the living room and kitchen, but cannot stand walking on cold floors in your bedroom. Or perhaps you have discovered that you have a better outlook on life when your bedroom window faces the sunrise. The list can go on and on, but I'm sure that you have already discovered some of your ideal amenities throughout your years of renting. That is a good source to draw from to put together a list of must-have features in your prospective home.

Here is a list to get you started:

General

House Style
Square footage
Number of bedrooms
Number of closets
Number of bathrooms
Garage
Ideal Home Age
Hardwood Floors or Carpet
Fireplace

Central Air

Updated house systems (plumbing, electrical or mechanical)

Floor Plan

Number of floors (two story, etc.)

Great room

Formal living room/dining room

Basement/Attic

Laundry room

Family/Den

Home office

Kitchen

Spacious or compact

Type of flooring

Granite vs. Butcher block

Eat-in

Automatic Dishwasher

Outside

Large yard/big lot

Small yard/small lot

Fenced in property

Pool/Spa

When you do decide which neighborhood you want to live in, view it in terms of neighborhood "niceties," as well as your neighborhood "exit strategy." These are the intangibles and tangibles that will make or break a neighborhood. Let's take a look:

"Niceties"

- **Convenience Factor** – How close are you to work, shopping centers, schools, grocery stores, etc? There is nothing worse than your gas needle being on "E" with no gas station in sight for twenty miles.
- **Welcoming Community** – You would not want to move into a community that views new residents as the devil incarnate. You want to feel that you are a great addition to the community.
- **Education Factor** – If you have kids, then you know how important being in a good school district is to your child.
- **Safety and Security** - Knowing that both you and your biggest investment are safe at all times lets you sleep at night.
- **Restricted Communities** – There are neighborhoods that require you to paint your house certain colors and restricts you from painting it any other color or pay a fine. Do you want to be that limited with your property?

"Exit Strategy"

If this is your first home - or even if it is not – when you are selecting a neighborhood, think about the resale value. By keeping the resale value in mind, this might be the difference between having your house on the market for weeks or months if and when you decide to sell your home.

The best way to determine resale value is to assess how well the intended house matches the neighborhood. For example, you don't want to own the only townhouse in a multi-family neighborhood. Chances are the majority of buyers who would be purchasing your home are looking for multi-family investment properties. The single-family homebuyer would feel like they are still renting and probably would not want to live in another transient renter's neighborhood.

Another method of putting together an exit strategy is to think about the very things you are looking for as a homebuyer: proximity to major highways, good schools, nearby shopping, clean streets, close to work, etc.

Your local Certified Affordable Housing Provider® is trained to find the property that is right for you. The number of bedrooms, the number of bathrooms, the location you prefer, special-needs that you may have such as handicap accessibility or an In-law suite. Be sure to tell them what you are looking for - And remember to tell them what is not acceptable to you.

You can easily provide this information online by going to your local CAHP's website. Find the web address inside the front cover or in their chapter included herein.

Chapter 5

Brand Spanking New Vs. Gently Used

Every single homebuyer that I have met has an image in their mind of what they want their home to be. Some want the traditional "white picket fence," while others dread any type of manual labor and elect to go with a professionally maintained condo community. But at the end of the day, the only thing that matters is that you choose a house that you and you alone can live with.

There are basically two groups of single family houses to choose from: "Brand New," and "Gently Used." Let's talk about the pros and cons of a "Brand New" house:

One of the best parts about buying a newly constructed house is that you are the first to make the house a *home* by leaving your own personal mark on it. Other benefits include:

- **Everything is Updated** – If you are a gadget loving person, you will have to restrain yourself from going crazy with all of the latest and greatest gadgets.
- **Custom Made Just For You** – The best part is that YOU designed it, so you are able to see your vision come to life.

- **Environmentally Friendly** – Most of the new homes are built to save energy and are made with better materials.

Now on the flip side, new construction does have its down side:

- **Pushy salespeople** – These people are hired by the builders to move these houses, so they tend to be very aggressive and anxious to sell.
- **You are breaking everything in** – Nothing has been tested for longer than thirty seconds, so there may be one or two issues with appliances, heaters, a/c unit, etc.
- **Patience is a virtue** – Statistics show that builders almost never finish homes on time, so be prepared.
- **Additional costs** – Because of inflation and cost of goods rising, it usually costs more to build a home than it does to buy that same home if it was already built.

"Gently Used" homes tend to have some unique benefits that many homebuyers really enjoy, such as:

- **Tested Construction** - The majority of homes generally have their issues in the first few years.
- **Stable Neighborhood** – The community has been built and is functioning before you move in.

- **Personality** – Homes seem to develop character over time as they age.
- **Better prices** – Older homes usually have lower sales prices.

Once again, there are down sides to buying an older home:

- **Less efficient** – Older homes do not preserve energy as well due to the new materials manufactured in recent years.
- **Costs of repairs** – Father Time has put his mark on appliances and materials, so they generally need to be repaired or replaced soon after moving in.
- **Smaller rooms** – At one time it was prestigious just to own a home, so size really didn't matter.
- **They usually sell for less later on** – Newer construction holds its value better.

Are Multi Family Units a Better Fit?

Single family and multi-family dwellings are as different as night and day. Even though most people are familiar with condos, did you know that there are three types of housing structures that are broken down into communities? This means that when you buy into a condo community there are certain responsibilities that the community at-large provides for you, and then there are certain responsibilities you perform for the community (usually in the way of paying their monthly fees).

There are three major types of multi-housing communities: Condominiums, Town Homes, and Co-Op Associations:

1) **Condominiums**

   When you buy a condo you own only the inside of your home, not the common areas such as swimming pools, stairwells, gardens or sidewalks. Those areas belong to everybody. But owning a condo can make sense:

   - **Less work for you** - the condo association takes care of regular upkeep and maintenance so you don't have to: no cleaning of pools, no shoveling snow, no mowing grass, etc.
   - **Being part of a community** – this can be a blessing or a curse, depending on your neighbors.
   - **Lower sales price** – depending on where you live, you may get a better deal on a condo than on a single-family house.

The "not-so-pleasant" side of living in a condo is:

- Fees must be paid each and every month or you get penalized with fines.
- "Big Brother" is always watching.
- If you paid less, you'll make less when you sell
- Over- the- top rules, regulations and fees

2) Townhomes

Whereas a condo can have upwards of 30 floors or more, a townhouse is generally an "attached" vertical single family home, with two to three floors. Buying a townhouse is actually buying more than a condo, so you should expect to pay more because with a townhouse you actually get a title of ownership to the building and the land that it sits on.

3) Co-Ops

When you buy a co-op you are really buying shares of a corporation that in turn owns the building you are living in. What this means is that you are actually renting from the corporation, and as a result are bound by rules that appear to be only one step removed from renting. As a result of buying shares of the corporation, not only are you required to vote in order to make any real changes, but you must also pay a monthly membership or maintenance fee. As a first-time homebuyer, I strongly suggest staying as far away from co-ops as possible.

Your local Certified Affordable Housing Provider® is familiar with all types of real estate and can find the housing type that is right for you.

Chapter 6

The Importance of Knowing and Maintaining Your Credit Scores

Most people are oblivious to how important their credit score truly is. You can't get a credit card (unless it's a Secured credit card) with a poor credit score. You can't buy a car with a poor credit score. And most importantly, your credit score will determine if you are eligible, or not, for a mortgage.

Now over the years I have heard so many people say, "I just pay everything with cash, so I don't need credit." Ah, if it were only true. Since credit scores reflect how you pay back money borrowed, the credit companies will not know how you pay your debts if you don't borrow any money. It's that old Catch 22 syndrome. Loan companies need some way to find out if you are a good credit risk or not. Would you loan your money to someone with little to no history of pay back? I doubt it. You would want to make sure you got paid back, and on time. The same goes for the lenders.

There are three major credit companies where lenders gather your information from, and they are:

- Experian FICO – Experian/Fair Isaac Risk Model®
- Equifax FICO – BEACON score®

- Transunion FICO – EMPIRICA®

These three major credit bureaus monitor the credit history that is listed on your credit reports. In some cases, information will stay on their report for up to ten years. What exactly do they look for? They check to make sure that you are paying your obligations on time and if not, how delinquent you are. They look at credit cards, bankruptcies, tax liens, bills, car loans, judgments, miscellaneous loans, foreclosures and credit inquiries. They even check to see if you have a credit record that will even generate a score.

Just how do they even calculate your credit score?

35% - payment history
30% - amounts owed
15% - length of credit history
10% - new credit
10% - type of credit use

Based on the above percentages, you can see how important it is to have the precise information on your scores before purchasing your home. In addition, let me dispel some myths about how credit bureaus calculate your scores:

1. Each credit bureau will have a different credit score. They each put a different importance

on individual factors.

2. Married couples do not share the same credit scores. Each individual is treated differently based on his or her own contributing factors.
3. Mortgage lenders use the middle score to qualify you for a mortgage and down payment program, and they do not average all of your scores together.

The Basics

Let's start with the basics of your personal credit score. Based on purchasing and payment history, your score can run from "won't touch you with a ten foot pole" score of 400 to a "whatever you want, you got" score of 850. Generally, to receive a decent mortgage, you average FICO® credit score should be above 620. But to receive the very best possible rates, a credit score of 720 and above is ideal.

Because your credit score gives lenders a close to perfect picture of your dependability, credibility and trustworthiness when it comes to paying your bills, they depend on the information from these companies to help determine the type of mortgage they can offer you. Let's say you have a score of 730. This would allow you to get a mortgage where the interest rate if far below the average rate, without paying extra fees like loan discount points.

Points are dollars that are either paid out of pocket or added to the amount financed. Say you want to borrow $200,000. One point would be $2,000 (200,000 x .01). This is extra money that you would need to pay to get your loan.

Maintaining a high credit score also means getting a par rate, which is the lowest interest rate you can qualify for *without* paying extra money to get it lower. Now you still might be able to qualify for a mortgage if your score is 620 or lower, but you will be penalized by paying interest of 2% to 6% above par. Why do they charge these extra rates? It protects the lenders from people who are bad credit risks.

Check out this credit score guide. Depending on your credit scores, this will give you an idea of what to expect from a mortgage lender:

720-higher	**A**	You get access to all down payment programs, the best interest rates for conventional, conforming and FHA or VA home financing, and expect to pay minimum costs for your mortgage.

620-719	**B**	You qualify for conventional, conforming and FHA or VA financing, but you are viewed as a slight credit risk. You should expect to pay a higher interest rate and slightly higher fees when getting a mortgage.
600-619	**C**	You are right on the bubble and getting a mortgage approval will require a manual review by an underwriter. You may not qualify for conventional or conforming, but FHA and VA may still be an option for you. You should expect to pay higher interest rates and higher loan fees.
575-599	**D**	Most lenders will deny your loan unless you are putting close to 20% down. You should also expect to pay a significantly higher interest rate and loan fees.
400-574	**F**	If you are here then it is time to go back to the drawing board and

regroup. You definitely need to get some help with increasing your scores before proceeding with purchasing a home.

The Minimums Allowed

To have your mortgage approved with the lowest fixed interest rate, the minimum middle credit score you will need from each of the three credit bureaus is 620. This will almost always automatically insure your loan approval from your mortgage lenders automated underwriting program. So for example, if you have a 601, 625 and 683, then a mortgage lender will use the 625 to determine whether you qualify for a specific first-time homebuyer program.

The mortgage professional who assists you with your mortgage will submit your application and credit reports through an automated underwriting or desktop underwriting system called DU. This computerized system will instantaneously review all of your information and notify the mortgage professional within seconds. The computerized system will give you one of three possible outcomes:

- **Approved** – Your credit scores are well above 620 and you are approved as long as your application, paystubs, W2's and all other supporting documentation are verified by an actual person. A live underwriter will then issue you a final approval.

- **Review** – Your credit scores are right around 620 or below and the automated underwriting system wants the underwriter to review it before issuing an approval or denial. This is the reason why most folks end up waiting several days before knowing if they are approved for a mortgage or not.
- **Denied** – Your credit scores are well below 620 and you also might have some challenges with meeting the income requirement. This means your application was not accepted and your mortgage professional, if he is a broker, will have the choice of going to a different lender. However, if he only works for one bank and does not have any other lenders, then you will have to go elsewhere for help.

If you are notified that your application is denied, don't be too discouraged. Many lenders will make exceptions when there are other good factors in your favor, such as a long employment history or $50,000 in your bank account. So don't give up hope until you talk with your mortgage professional.

Overcoming Credit Challenges

The majority of people are not even aware that they have issues with their credit reports until it is too late. Did you know that almost half of the American population has incorrect information on their credit reports? Most credit is denied because information is computer driven. This is why some lenders will let customers look at their credit report when they are applying and submit a written explanation to any discrepancies. Some may even help you try and fix the problems!

Here are a few of the most common errors on a credit report:

- Loans you never took out
- Identity theft
- Erroneous late payments
- Bankruptcies, foreclosures, tax liens and other judgments that have been completed, satisfied or discharged but never changed to reflect the status on the report
- Credit cards that were never used, but are still showing as being open
- Credit cards and debts that do not belong to you
- Former spouses that are still carrying the other's line of credit on their reports.

The Path To Home Ownership

There comes a time in everyone's life when we want to make a big purchase, such as a car or a house. So be prepared ahead of time with knowing that your credit scores are in order. Here are a few steps that will help you increase and improve your credit scores:

1. **Purchase your official FICO® credit scores**
   The scores that the "Big 3" give you are not the same credit scores that lenders use, so be sure to purchase the official FICO® credit scores. This will give you the same report that the lenders get, along with the top 12 reasons why your score is what it is. And buy it every 90 days. This will give you the updates you need to be sure that all the negative stuff is taken care of.
2. **Sign-up with a credit monitoring service that advises you instantly by email and text message any time there is a change on your credit reports.**
   Subscribe to a credit monitoring service that will let you know immediately via text and email whenever there is a change to your credit reports, whether positive or negative.
3. **Hire an expert credit repair company**
   I recommend anyone who has a low credit score and several negative accounts to seriously look into having a professional help you repair your credit scores. They know what they are doing. But

just keep in mind that during this process do not make any new unnecessary bills (like opening a new credit card), and pay your bills on time.

4. **Don't get discouraged!**
   You didn't ruin your credit overnight, so what makes you think you can repair it with one simple phone call? It can take four to six months to repair and increase your scores. So have patience, and know that the result will be life-changing.

If you decide to do it on your own without the help of an expert:

a) Request your reports from the "Big 3"
b) Find the items you need to dispute
c) Write dispute letters to each of the bureaus
d) Ask the credit bureau to investigate your claim and remove the incorrect information
e) Ask for an updated copy of your report
f) Review your report bi-annually to be sure it is correct and up-to-date.

Quick Tips To Immediately Increase Your Credit Scores

Before, during and after you purchase your home, work on increasing your credit scores:

- Pay your bills early or on time
- Know all three of your scores

- Use credit instead of cash
- Maintain a few major credit cards
- Do not max out credit cards each month
- Pay down debt instead of shifting it
- Stay away from finance companies
- Apply for credit at the right time
- Use the credit you have
- Pay off your credit cards each month
- Do not co-sign for another person
- Bank/Debit cards won't help your credit rating
- Eliminate mistakes on your credit reports
- Increase your credit limits regularly
- Ignore preapproved offers in the mail

To make it simple and easy for you, your local Certified Affordable Housing Provider® will collect a credit report fee from you, or refer you to or give you a link to a reputable mortgage lender we have identified who is completely familiar with our programs and will pull your credit report and provide a full credit analysis, including how long they think it will be before you are able to qualify for a loan.

Don't be surprised if they come back and say you are ready now. Many people who apply for our Path To Home Ownership® program actually have good enough credit to qualify for a loan now.

Simply contact your local CAHP identified in this book to get going right away.

Chapter 7

Financing and Bank Loan Possibilities

Most people believe you must have a pile of money in order to buy a home. There are a number of reasons why this is not true. For example:

VA Financing - if you are a veteran, you could get 100% financing. That means zero down. Whoa, don't get too excited yet. You still will need to pay some of the closing costs and you will need credit good enough to qualify. But regardless of your credit, be sure and tell your affordable housing counselor that you were a veteran. They will use this information to help you seek the right loan. The Veteran's Administration does not actually loan money. It acts as a guarantor for the loan. Qualified mortgage lenders provide the loan.

If you can qualify for an FHA loan you only need 3.5% down payment. So that's only $3,500 on a $100,000 loan. Not bad. But once again you will need good enough credit in order to qualify. The program requirements and credit scores change regularly, so our Mortgage Wiz can tell you what score you will need in order to qualify for an FHA loan today.

Once again, the federal home association is not a lender. It insures the loan and the added risk a lender is taking with such a small down payment. Therefore, on this type of loan, there is an added fee payable to FHA. This insurance premium is called MIP, for Mortgage Insurance Premium.

As we progress through the list of possibilities, the pile of money needed to be able to purchase increases.
The next possibility could be a conventional loan. These are available for up to 95% of the purchase price. When borrowing more than 80% of the purchase price of a home, often lenders want insurance. This is called MPI, for Mortgage Premium Insurance.

80 to 90% of purchase price is most common when it comes to conventional financing. Again, a good enough credit history and score is needed to qualify for this type of loan.

Even with a poor credit score most lenders will lend 70% of the purchase price of the home.

All of the above are related to traditional bank lending. As noted, good credit and/or sufficient down payment is required.

For those of you who don't have that just yet, there are other options available.

In some cases the seller of the property will act as your

bank. If the seller has equity in their property, they can lend that equity – not money – but the equity in the property to you. They will typically charge an interest rate and require payments over a certain period of time. The interest rate typically relates to the risk the lender is taking. If you have poor or damaged credit then expect to pay a rate higher than the bank charges for 'A' credit borrowers.

Until you have good enough credit and/or a down payment, then your local Certified Affordable Housing Provider® can place you on the Path To Home Ownership to help you get a place to live in while you are building up the necessary requirements for a bank loan.

Your local CAHP will help navigate these options and help you choose the one that's right for you in your current situation.

Chapter 8

Sweat Equity and Other Down Payment Assistance

Lots of people have the motivation to buy a home, but just don't have enough down payment money saved up.

Often buyers think they need more than they really do. In any case, the more down payment you have, the lower your monthly payments are going to be.

So let's take a look at possible places you can add to the amount of down payment money you have to work with:

1) **Government down payment assistance.** City, County and State programs are available to assist. The requirements and restrictions vary widely. Ask the mayor’s office or local housing office what may be available in your area. Many of these programs are poorly publicized, so only those who seek them out get to take advantage of them. Your local CAHP should be up to date on any programs you can access. It's hard for anyone to know them all, so feel free to do your own research as well because there are so many, and they come and go regularly.

2) **Non-profit organization down payment assistance.** Some provide home ownership training programs, including budgeting and home maintenance. Some also provide down payment assistance once you complete certain training classes. Again, this will take research to discover what's available now.
3) **Family down payment assistance.** Also known as gifts. Many want to see family members get ahead and will gift or lend some or all the down payment needed. Have you asked? Grandparents, parents, uncles, aunts, siblings and friends are often sources of added down payment, as they want to see their loved ones get ahead. If you don't ask - you often don't get.
4) **Employer down payment assistance.** Some employers grant loans or gifts to assist employees to buy a home. Be sure to ask your employer if they offer such a program, and get the requirement details.
5) **Retirement Account down payment assistance.** Your Individual Retirement Account (IRA) or 401k account could be a source, depending on how your employer has drafted the account language. Often these funds can be accessed for a loan at a very low interest rate.

6) **Work For Equity down payment booster.** One of my favorite down payment assistance grants is to allow a Path To Home Ownership® buyer or renter to do some or all of any needed work on a select property. Earn valuable credit towards your move-in fee or down payment. The process is quick and easy. Your local CAHP will provide a list of items that need to be done to the house you choose from their inventory or one they find for you. You simply review the list and check off the items you or family members and friends can do. Your CAHP will assess a value to these items and offer that amount as a credit towards your down payment. What could be easier? Engage family and friends, apply a bit of elbow grease and earn a fat credit to build up your down payment.
7) **Life Insurance.** Some life insurance policies allow for borrowing at very low rates. This is a perfect place to access extra down payment funds.
8) **After Move in - keep building.** As a Path To Home Ownership® client you can earn extra credit every month towards building up credits to build you down payment. For example, at the Silver level (Rent To Own program) every month that you pay on time you earn a credit towards your down payment.

9) **Extra monthly payments down payment credits.** Commit part of your paycheck to building up your down payment to move to the next level on your Path To Home Ownership®.

Accounting for these or other grants, gifts or loans should be done with care in consultation with your Certified Affordable Housing Provider® as these funds must be properly sourced and seasoned to be recognized as legitimate down payments by traditional lenders.

Combine as many of the above opportunities as possible and boost your down payment. Remember - the more you put down, the lower your monthly payment will be.

Chapter 9

Steps to Home Ownership

Whether you are a first time home buyer, interested in owner financing, have bad credit, perfect credit, or maybe no credit at all, we have programs to help you achieve your ultimate dream of home ownership.

Our programs are designed to start you based on what you can afford today and support you as you grow to eventual home ownership... if YOU choose.

Start Your Path to Home Ownership™

As a rental client you enter our Bronze Level. As a Rent to Own client you become a Silver Level member. As an in-house financing client you become a Gold Level member, and as someone who can qualify for new bank financing you earn Platinum Member status.

As a local Certified Affordable Housing Provider® we are equipped to help you grow at your own pace.

Below are a variety of programs that can meet your needs. Each step up the Path To Home Ownership® offers added bonuses and benefits. Qualifying for any level depends on the amount you have to put down. The platinum level (home ownership) requires a good credit score.

Whether you have income, credit, or location challenges, we offer options to earn and build credit toward home ownership. Based on combined household income, anyone with good, fair or poor credit can qualify. We have programs that fit large, medium or small initial down payments.

An unfortunate reality of today's economy is that many people can't qualify for traditional bank loans. This prevents many good honest and hardworking individuals from achieving their dream of home ownership. Owner financed homes are home loans that are provided by the owner, rather than a bank. This helps you to build the credit and equity you need to eventually qualify for a bank loan and own your home outright.

If you don't have enough down payment to qualify for a new home, you can join our VIP program. This is our 'House on Layaway' plan, where you deposit with us the initial funds you have to work with now, and contribute more each pay period until you accumulate enough to move in.

Let's take a quick look at our multi-level program:

1) **Bronze Level - Rent**

Whether you're just starting out or you need affordable, reliable housing for your growing family, our Certified Affordable Housing Providers® may currently have a number of homes for rent in your area. There are a number of reasons why you should consider renting your next home or apartment through our Path to Home Ownership® program. Unlike traditional landlords, our focus isn't on simply profiting from your monthly rent checks. Our goal is to provide our customers with homes for rent that they can eventually call their own. The Path to Home Ownership® program was designed to help consumers find quality affordable housing at any level, and to help you move through the program steps towards your goal of eventual home ownership. Even renters are given a plan to follow and the opportunity of eventually owning their own home. Why rent someone else's home when you can own the home you're renting?

2) **Silver Level – Rent To Own Program**

Our Rent to Own option gives prospective homeowners the opportunity to obtain housing now while they work towards repairing credit issues and building the necessary down payments needed to qualify for a traditional bank loan.

With a small down payment you can actually move into your home now and earn a fixed monthly credit towards the ultimate purchase of your new home. Once you've improved your credit standing and down payment situation you can easily move into our Owner Financing program, or straight to a traditional low interest bank loan and own the exact home you've been living in.

The PTHO Rent to Own program is perfect for those people with credit issues or who haven't been able to save a down payment yet, but want to start building towards home ownership now. Additionally, this program is excellent for those who have just moved to a new area and simply want to test out the neighborhood before committing to a home purchase.

3) **Gold Level – Owner Financed Home Program**
Path to Home Ownership® Gold level members are eligible for our in-house financing program. This program affords alternative financing to individuals and families looking to purchase their own home now. Our Certified Affordable Housing Providers® are trained to examine and evaluate every one of our customer's unique situations

and needs to create their own individual Path to Home Ownership® based on the level of payment you can afford and sustain long term. Our Gold level members enjoy money saving tax deductions, while building their credit score towards a traditional low interest bank loan. We even place our Gold level customers with qualified and experienced mortgage professionals to help find the right mortgage for your individual needs. Our goal is to help our customers achieve the reality of home ownership sooner, and put our customers on the path to long term financial success with their home.

4) **Platinum Level – Traditional Home Sales**
The Path to Home Ownership®program wasn't designed simply for renters looking to start down the Path to Home Ownership®. Our program was designed to help home buyers at any level achieve quality, affordable housing for their family. We have hundreds of homes available for purchase today to qualified buyers. We can help you work with the mortgage companies to obtain the best possible mortgage program for you, and move you into your new home faster.

Whether you are a renter, first time home buyer, or

have owned several homes before, the Path to Home Ownership® program was designed to provide you with the best opportunity to obtain your own home. If you have credit or financial issues that need to be resolved prior to purchasing, or if you are ready to apply for a traditional bank or FHA loan now, we have the right program to help get you into the home of your dreams right away.

Find A Local CAHP Agent

Certified Affordable Housing Providers® simply find and offer housing that matches what a person or family can afford. Whether it's a house for rent or a lease purchase, we have options for you.

How is that different than what Landlords do?
Landlords give tenants housing, but provide no future path for that tenant to eventually own a home. Believing that home ownership advances the person, the family, and society in a positive way, Certified Affordable Housing Providers® offer a plan to allow their clients to advance and grow into home ownership.

Certified Affordable Housing Providers® serve your local community in many ways...

- Stabilize communities by purchasing vacant, and therefore crime-attracting, properties.

- Benefit the economy by hiring people and buying supplies locally, then restoring properties and returning them to the local property and school tax rolls.
- Support the environment by using the GREEN housing concept of recycling existing structures, rather than tearing down and building new.
- Serve families and individuals by offering housing to deserving families to buy now or sometime in the future.
- Save resources as much of this is accomplished without government funding.

These powerful and life-changing benefits for families, the community and government are provided by hard working entrepreneurs and non-profits groups.

Bonus Chapter

Important Real Estate Terms

Adjustable Rate Mortgage (ARM): Mortgage loans under which the interest rate is periodically adjusted to more closely coincide are agreed to at the inception of the loan.

Alternative Documentation: The use of pay stubs, W-2 forms, and bank statements in lieu of Verifications of Employment (VOE) and Verifications of Deposit (VOD) to qualify a borrower for a mortgage.

Amortization: The systematic and continuous payment of an obligation through installments until the debt has been paid in full.

Annual Percentage Rate (APR): A term used in the Truth-in-Lending Act to present the percentage relationship of the total finance charge to the amount of the loan. The APR reflects the cost of the mortgage loan as a yearly rate. It could be higher than the interest rate stated on the Note because it includes, in addition to the interest rate, loan discount points, miscellaneous fees and mortgage insurance.

Appraisal: A report made by a qualified person setting forth an opinion or estimate of property value.

(Appraisal also refers to the process through which a conclusion on property value is derived.)

Appraisal Amount or Appraised Value: The fair market value of a home determined by an independent appraisal. The appraisal uses local real estate market sales activity as a major basis for valuation.

Appreciation: An increase in the value of a property due to market conditions or other causes. The opposite is depreciation.

Balloon Mortgage: A fixed-rate mortgage for a set number of years which then must be paid off in full in a single "balloon" payment. Balloon loans are popular with borrowers expecting to sell or refinance their property within a definite period of time.

Bankruptcy: Legal relief from the payment of all debts after the surrender of all assets to a court-appointed trustee. Assets are distributed to creditors as full satisfaction of debts, with certain priorities and exemptions. A person, firm or corporation may declare bankruptcy under one of several chapters of the U. S. Bankruptcy Code: Chapter 7 covers liquidation of the debtor's assets; Chapter 11 covers reorganization of bankrupt businesses; Chapter 13 covers payment of debts by individuals through a bankruptcy plan.

Cap: The limit placed on adjustments that can be made to the interest rate or payments, such as the annual cap on an adjustable rate loan (ARM) or the cap on a rate over the life of the loan.

Cash-out Refinance: To refinance the mortgage on a property for more than the principal owed. This allows the borrower to get cash from the equity in their home. Loan products may vary on how much can be borrowed on a cash-out refinance.

Certified Mortgage Specialist (CMS): The Certified Mortgage Specialist is the professional sales associate who communicates the needs of the agent and borrower to the operation team.

Client Coordinator (CC): The Client Coordinator sets the tone throughout the application process and ensures that each customer is kept informed of all needs and status through clear and concise communication.

Closer: The person who coordinates the closing time with the Client Coordinator and reviews and prepares the necessary closing documents.

Closing: Also known as settlement, the finalization of the process of purchasing or refinancing real estate. The closing includes the delivery of a Deed, the signing of Notes and the disbursement of funds.

Closing Costs: Costs that are due at closing, in addition to the purchase price of the property. These costs normally include, but are not limited to, origination fee, discount points, attorney's fees, costs for title insurance, surveys, recording documents, and prepayment of real estate taxes and insurance premiums held by the lender. Sometimes the seller will help the borrower pay some of these costs.

Closing Statement: An accounting of the debits and credits incurred at closing. All FHA, VA and Conventional financing loans use a Uniform Closing or Settlement Statement commonly referred to as the HUD-1.

Co-Borrower: A party who signs the mortgage note along with the primary borrower, and who also shares title to the subject real estate.

Collateral: Property pledged as security for a debt. For example, real estate that secures a mortgage. Collateral can be repossessed if the loan is not repaid.

Combined Loan To Value (CLTV): The mathematical relationship between the total of all loan amounts (first mortgage plus subordinate liens) and the value of the subject property.

Community Reinvestment Act (CRA): This act requires financial institutions to meet the credit needs of their community, including low and moderate-income sections of the local community. It also requires banks to make reports concerning their investment in the areas where they do business.

Condominium: A form of property ownership in which the homeowner holds title to an individual dwelling unit, an undivided interest in common areas of a multi-unit project, and sometimes the exclusive use of certain limited common areas. All condominiums must meet certain investor requirements.

Conforming Loan: A loan with a mortgage amount that does not exceed that which is eligible for purchase by FNMA or FHLMC. All loans are considered either as conforming or non-conforming, also known as jumbo.

Conventional Loan: A mortgage loan not insured or guaranteed by the federal government.

Conversion Option: Options to convert an adjustable rate mortgage or balloon loan to a fixed rate mortgage under specified conditions.

Co-Signer: A party who signs the mortgage note along with the borrower, but who does not own or have any interest in the title to the property.

Creditor: A person to whom debt is owed by another person who is the "debtor."

Credit Rating: A rating given a person or company to establish credit-worthiness based upon present financial condition, experience and past credit history.

Credit Report: A document completed by a credit-reporting agency providing information about the buyer's credit cards, previous mortgage history, bank loans and public records dealing with financial matters.

Deal Structure: An Underwriters review of certain aspects of a loan application that do not meet standard guidelines.

Debt to Income Ratio: Compares the amount of monthly income to the amount the borrower will owe each month in house payment (PITI) plus other debts. The other debts may include, but not limited to, car payment, credit cards, alimony, child support, and personal loans. This ratio is commonly used to see if the borrower has the capacity to repay the debt.

Deed of Trust: A legal document that conveys title to real estate to a disinterested third party (trustee) who holds the title until the owner of the property has repaid the debt. In states where it is used, a Deed of Trust accomplishes essentially the same purpose as a Mortgage.

Default: Failure to comply with the terms of any agreement. In real estate, generally used in connection with a mortgage obligation to refer to the failure to comply with the terms of the Promissory Note. Most often this default is a failure to make payments. However, there are other means by which a borrower may default, such as the failure to pay real estate taxes.

Depreciation: A decline in the value of property. The opposite of appreciation.

Discount Points: A percentage of the loan amount which is charged or credited by the lender upon making a mortgage loan. Loans that are made at the present market rate, with no points, are considered to be made at "par." Because of the lender's ability to charge or credit points on an individual loan, the lender is able to tailor a loan program and interest rate to fit the needs of each individual borrower. Discount points can be negotiated in the Purchase Contract to be paid by either the seller or the borrower.

Each point equals 1% of the mortgage loan. For example, a charge of 1 point on a $50,000 loan would result in a charge of $500; 1/2 point would be $250 ($50,000 x .50%).

Down Payment: The part of the purchase price which the buyer pays in cash and does not finance with a mortgage.

Earnest Money: Deposit made by a purchaser of real estate as evidence of good faith.

Equal Credit Opportunity Act (ECOA): Also known as Regulation B. A federal law that prohibits a lender from discriminating in mortgage lending on the basis of race, color, religion, national origin, sex, marital status, age, income derived from public assistance programs, or previous exercise of Consumer Credit Protection Act rights.

Equity: The difference between the current market value of a property and the principal balance of all outstanding loans.

Escrow Account: An account held by the lending institution to which the borrower pays monthly installments for property taxes, insurance, and special assessments, and from which the lender disburses these sums as they become due.

Fair Credit Reporting Act: Regulating the collection and distribution of information by the consumer credit reporting industry. It also affects how financial institutions collect and convey credit information about loan applicants or borrowers.

Fair Housing Act: Prohibits the denial or variance of the terms of real estate related transactions based on race, color, religion, sex, national origin, disability, or familiar status of the credit applicant. Real estate related transactions include a mortgage, home improvement, or other loans secured by a dwelling.

Federal Home Loan Mortgage Corporation (FHLMC): Also known as Freddie Mac. A publicly owned corporation created by Congress to support the secondary mortgage market. It purchases and sells conventional residential mortgages, as well as residential mortgages insured by the Federal Housing Administration (FHA), or guaranteed by the Veterans Administration (VA).

Federal National Mortgage Association (FNMA): Also known as Fannie Mae. A privately owned corporation to support the secondary mortgage market. It adds liquidity to the mortgage market by investing in home loans through the country.

FICO Score: A credit score given to a person that establishes creditworthiness based on present financial condition, experience and past credit history.

Finance Charge: The cost of credit as a dollar amount (i.e. total amount of interest and specific other loan charges to be paid over the term of the loan and other loan charges to be paid by the borrower at closing). Loan charges include origination fees, discount points, mortgage insurance, and other applicable charges. If the seller pays any of these charges, they cannot be included in the finance charge.

Financial Statement: A summary of facts showing an individual's or company's financial condition. For individuals, it states their assets and liabilities as of a given date. For a company, it should include a Profit and Loss Statement (P&L) for a certain period of time and balance sheet, stating assets and liabilities as of a given date.

First Mortgage: A real estate loan that creates a primary lien against real property.

First Rate Adjustment -- First rate adjustment after: In association with an Adjustable Rate Mortgage loan, this is the number of months after which the loan has closed when the first interest rate adjustment will occur.

First Rate Adjustment -- Maximum rate decrease: In association with an Adjustable Rate Mortgage loan, this is the most the interest rate can decrease during the first adjustment period.

First Rate Adjustment -- Maximum rate increase: In association with an Adjustable Rate Mortgage loan, this is the most the interest rate can increase during the first adjustment period.

Fixed Rate Mortgage: The type of loan where the interest rate will not change for the entire term of the loan.

Floating: The term used when a purchaser elects not to lock-in an interest rate at the time of application.

Flood Insurance: Insurance that compensates for direct physical damages by or from flood to the insured property subject to the terms, provisions, conditions and losses not covered in the provision of the policy. It is required for mortgages on properties located in federally designated flood areas.

Good Faith Estimate (GFE): An estimate of settlement charges paid by the borrower at closing. The Real Estate Settlement Procedures Act (RESPA) requires a Good Faith Estimate of settlement charges be provided to the borrower.

Gift Letter: A letter or affidavit that indicates that part of a borrower's down payment is supplied by relatives or friends in the form of a gift, and that the gift does not have to be repaid.

Gross Income: A person's income before deduction for income taxation.

Hazard Insurance: Insurance against losses caused by perils which are commonly covered in policies described as a "Homeowner Policy."

Home Maintenance: Costs associated with maintaining a home. This may include, but not limited to, general repairs, replacement or repair of furnace, air conditioning, roof, plumbing and electrical systems.

Home Mortgage Disclosure Act (HMDA): Also known as

Regulation C. The purpose of HMDA is to provide disclosure of mortgage lending application activity (home purchase or improvement) to regulators and the public. Information is collected on each application, and is recorded on a log that is compiled to produce a report on application activity by geographic designation (census tract).

Homeowners Association (HOA): A non-profit corporation or association that manages common areas and services of a Condominium or Planned Unit Development (PUD).

Homeowners Insurance: Insurance that covers damage to the insured's residence and liability claims made against the insured subject to the policy terms, conditions, provisions, losses not insured provision and exclusions.

Housing Expense Ratio: Ratio used to determine the borrowers capacity to repay a home loan. The ratio compares monthly income to the house payment (Principal, Interest, Taxes and Insurance).

Index: In connection with ARM loans, the external measurement used by a Lender to determine future changes which are to occur to an adjustable loan program. These will typically be published rates that are independent of the Lender's control, such as a Treasury Bill.

Initial Interest Rate: The beginning interest rate at the start of an adjustable rate mortgage (ARM). It may be lower than the fully indexed rate or "going market rate," and it will remain constant until it is adjusted up or down on the adjustment date.

Interest: The amount paid by a borrower to a lender for the use of the lender's money for a certain period of time. The amount paid by a bank on some deposit accounts.

Interest Income: The potential income from funds which would have been used for the down payment, closing costs, and any difference (increase) between monthly rental payment and monthly mortgage payment.

Interest Rate: The percentage of an amount of money that is paid for its use for a specific time; usually expressed as an annual percentage.

Judgment: Decree of a court declaring that one individual is indebted to another and fixing the amount of such indebtedness.

Jumbo Loan: A loan above the limit set by the Federal National Mortgage Association (Fannie Mae) and the Federal Home Loan Mortgage Corporation (Freddie Mac). Also referred to as a non-conforming loan.

Late Charge: An additional charge a borrower is required to pay as a penalty for failure to pay a regular mortgage loan installment when due; a penalty for a delinquent payment.

Lien: A legal claim against a property that must be paid off when the property is sold. A lien is created when you borrow money and use your home as collateral for the loan.

Life of Loan -- Maximum rate decrease: In association with an Adjustable Rate Mortgage loan, this is the most the interest can decrease over the life of the mortgage loan.

Life of Loan -- Maximum rate increase: In association with an Adjustable Rate Mortgage loan, this is the most the interest can increase over the life of the mortgage loan.

Loan Application: A source of information on which the lender bases a decision to make or not make a loan; defines the terms of the loan contract, gives the names of the borrower(s), place of employment, salary, bank accounts, credit references, real estate owned, and describes the property to be mortgaged.

Loan Balance: The amount of remaining unpaid principal balance owed by the borrower.

Loan Term: Number of years a loan is amortized. Mortgage loan terms are generally 15, 20, or 30 years.

Loan-to-Value (LTV): The ratio of the total amount borrowed on a mortgage against a property, compared to the appraised value of the property. A LTV ratio of 90 means that the borrower is borrowing 90% of the value of the property and paying 10% as a down payment. For purchases, the value of the property is the lesser of the purchase price or the appraised value. For refinances the value is determined by an appraisal.

Loan-to-Value Ratio: The ratio, expressed as a percentage, of the amount of the loan (numerator) to the value or selling price of real property (denominator). For example, if you have an $80,000 1st mortgage on a home with an appraised value of $100,000, the LTV is 80% ($80,000 / $100,000 = 80%).

Lock-In: A written agreement between the lender and borrower for a specified period of time in which the lender will hold a specific interest rate, origination and/or discount point(s).

Margin: Under the terms of an adjustable rate mortgage (ARM), the margin is a set adjustment to the index. The particular loan product determines the amount of the margin.

Median Income: The middle income level. Half of the incomes would be higher than the median income and half of the incomes would be below the median income. This is not to be confused with an average income.

Mortgage: The written instrument used to pledge a title to real estate as security for repayment of a Promissory Note.

Mortgage Insurance: Insurance written in connection with a mortgage loan that indemnifies the lender in the event of borrower default. In connection with conventional loan transactions, this insurance is commonly referred to as Private Mortgage Insurance (PMI).

Mortgage Note: A written promise to pay a sum of money at a stated interest rate during a specified term. It is typically secured by a mortgage.

Mortgage Servicing: Controlling the necessary duties of a mortgagee, such as collecting payments, releasing the lien upon payment in full, foreclosing if in default, and making sure the taxes are paid, insurance is in force, etc. The lender or a company acting for the lender, for a servicing fee, may do servicing. (Also called Loan Servicing.)

Mortgagee: The institution, group, or individual that lends money on the security of pledged real estate; the association, the lender.

Mortgagee Clause: This is the clause that is typically used for hazard insurance and flood insurance. For loans originated by the State Farm Bank it will read: State Farm Bank, F.S.B., Its Successor and/or Assigns, P.O. Box 2583, Ft. Wayne, IN 46801-2583.

Mortgagor: The owner of real estate who pledges his property as security for the repayment of a debt; the borrower.

Net Income: The difference between effective gross income and expense, including taxes and insurance. The term is qualified as net income before depreciation and debt.

Non-Conforming: A loan with a mortgage amount that

exceeds that which is eligible for purchase by FNMA or FHLMC. All other loans above this amount are considered to be non-conforming or jumbo loans.

Non-Owner-Occupied Property: Property purchased by a borrower not for a primary residence, but as an investment with the intent of generating rental income, tax benefits, and profitable resale.

Note: A written promise by one party to pay a specific sum of money to a second party under conditions agreed upon mutually. Also called "promissory note."

Note Rate: The interest rate on the mortgage loan.

Origination Fee: A fee paid to a lender for processing a loan application; it is stated as a percentage of the mortgage amount.

Origination Process: Process in which a lender solicits business, gathers required information and commits to loan money, for the purchase of real estate.

Owner-Occupied Property: The borrower or a member of the immediate family lives in the property as a primary residence.

PITI: Term commonly used to refer to a mortgage loan

payment. Acronym stands for Principal, Interest, Taxes, and Insurance.

PITI Ratio: Compares the amount of the monthly income to the amount the borrower will owe each month in principal, interest, real estate tax and insurance on a mortgage. Lenders use it in deciding whether to give the borrower a loan. Also called "income-to-debt" ratio.

Planned Unit Development (PUD): A housing project that may consist of any combination of homes (one-family to four-family), condominiums, and various other styles. In a PUD, often the individual unit and the land upon which it sits are owned by the unit/homeowner; however, the homeowner's association owns common facilities.

Pre-Approval: A process in which a customer provides appropriate information on income, debts and assets that will be used to make a credit only loan decision. The customer typically has not identified a property to be purchased, however a specific sales price and loan amount are used to make a loan decision. (The sales price and loan amount are based on customer assumptions)

Pre-Qualification: A process designed to assist a customer in determining a maximum sales price, loan amount and PITI payment they are qualified for. A pre-qualification is not considered a loan approval. A customer would provide basic information (income, debts, assets, et all) to be used to determine the maximum sales price, etc.

Prepaid Expenses or Prepaids: The term used to describe the funds the Lender requires to be deposited to establish the escrow account for taxes and insurance at the time of closing (also refers to Prepaid Interest).

Prepaid Interest: Interest that the borrower pays the lender before it becomes due.

Prepayment: A loan repayment made in advance of its contractual due date.

Prepayment Penalty: A penalty under a Note, Mortgage or Deed of Trust imposed when the loan is paid before its maturity date.

Principal and Interest: Two components of a monthly mortgage payment. Principal refers to the portion of the monthly payment that reduces the remaining balance for the mortgage. Interest is the fee charged for borrowing money.

Principal Balance: The outstanding balance of a mortgage, not counting interest.

Principal, Interest, Real Estate Tax, Insurance Payment: The total mortgage payment which includes principal, interest, taxes and insurance.

Private Mortgage Insurance (PMI): Insurance against a loss by a lender in the event of default by a borrower (mortgagor). A private insurance company issues this insurance. The premium is paid by the borrower and is included in the mortgage payment.

Processing: Gathering the loan application and all required supporting documents (including the property appraisal, credit report, credit history, and income and expenses) so that a lender can consider the borrower for a loan.

Promissory Note: A document in which the borrower promises to pay a stated amount on a specific date. The note normally states the name of the lender, the terms of payment and any interest rate.

Property Taxes: Taxes assessed on real estate. Property taxes are based on valuations by local and or state governments.

Purchase Agreement: A written agreement between a buyer and seller of real property which states the price and terms of the sale.

Purchase Price: The total amount paid for a home.

Qualifying Income Ratios: Income analysis used by lenders in deciding whether to offer the borrower a loan. One type of analysis compares only the amount of the proposed monthly mortgage payment to the monthly income. Another compares the amount of the total monthly payments (for example car, credit card and proposed mortgage payments) to the monthly income.

Rate Index: An index used to adjust the interest rate of an adjustable mortgage loan.

Real Estate Appreciation Rate: Percentage increase in the value of real estate, expressed at an annual rate.

Real Estate Settlement Procedures Act (RESPA): A consumer protection law that requires, among other things, lenders to give borrowers advance notice of closing costs.

Realtor: A person licensed to negotiate and transact the sale of real estate on behalf of the property owner. A real estate broker or associate must hold active membership in a real estate board affiliated with the National Association of Realtors.

Recording Fee: The amount paid to the recorder's office in order to make a document a matter of public record.

Regulation Z: Federal Reserve regulation issued under the Truth-in-Lending Act, which, among other things, requires that a credit purchaser be advised in writing of all costs connected with the credit portion of the loan.

Rental Payment: A payment made to use another's property. The amount of the rent is determined in a contract and is typically paid monthly.

Renters Insurance: Insurance against perils which are commonly covered in policies described as a "Renters Policy."

Repayment: The payment of a mortgage loan over a period of time established when the loan is originated.

Rescind: To avoid or cancel in such a way as to treat the contract or other object of the rescission as if it never existed.

Sales Contract: A written agreement between parties stating all terms and conditions of a sale.

Savings Rate: The interest rate a person expects to earn on a savings account or investment account.

Secondary Market: An informal market where existing mortgages are bought and sold. It is the traditional aftermarket for mortgage loans that brings together lenders that sell mortgages with lenders, investors and agencies that buy mortgages.

Seller Contribution: The seller may be paying some or all of the borrower's cost. The amount of the contribution has limitations.

Selling Costs: The costs incurred in selling a home. This could include Realtor expenses and other miscellaneous expenses such as painting or minor repairs to prepare the home for sale.

Servicing: All the management and operational procedures that the mortgage company handles for the life of the loan, up through foreclosure if necessary, including: collecting the mortgage payments, ensuring that the taxes and insurance charges are paid promptly, and sending an annual report on the mortgage and escrow accounts.

Servicing Released: A stipulation in the agreement for the sale of mortgages in which the Lender is not responsible for servicing the loan.

Servicing Retained: A loan sale in which the original lender's servicing department continues to service the loan after the sale to a secondary institution or investor.

Settlement Statement: Also referred to as a HUD-1 Settlement Statement. The complete breakdown of costs involved in the real estate transaction for both the seller and buyer.

Single-Family Attached Home: A single-family dwelling that is attached to other single-family dwellings.

Single-Family Detached Home: A freestanding dwelling for a single family.

Survey: A measurement of land, prepared by a registered land surveyor, showing the location of the land with reference to known points, its dimensions and the location and dimensions of any improvements.

Subordinate Financing: An additional lien against the real estate, securing the borrowers first mortgage. This lien takes second priority to the first mortgage.

Subsequent Rate Adjustment -- Maximum rate decrease: In association with an Adjustable Rate

Mortgage loan, this is the most the interest rate can decrease when it is scheduled for reevaluation and possible adjustment.

Subsequent Rate Adjustment -- Maximum rate increase: In association with an Adjustable Rate Mortgage loan, this is the most the interest rate can increase when it is scheduled for reevaluation and possible adjustment.

Subsequent Rate Adjustment -- Next ARM Adjustment Date: In association with an Adjustable Rate Mortgage loan, this is the date scheduled for the next reevaluation and possible adjustment.

Subsequent Rate Adjustment -- Rate Change Frequency: In association with an Adjustable Rate Mortgage loan, this is the frequency in which possible adjustments may be made to the interest rate amount for Adjustable Rate Mortgages after the initial adjustment.

Tax Rates: Tax levied by the federal government and some states based on a person's income. Federal income tax rates vary depending on a person's adjusted gross income.

Tax Savings: The amount saved on taxes by itemizing

deductions on income tax returns.

Title: The evidence to the right to or ownership in property. In the case of real estate, the documentary evidence of ownership is the title deed, which specifies in whom the legal state is vested and the history of ownership and transfers. Title may be acquired through purchase, inheritance, devise, gift, or through the foreclosure of a mortgage.

Title Insurance Policy: A contract by which the insurer, usually a title company, indicates who has legal title and agrees to pay the insured a specific amount of any loss caused by clouds, claims or defects of title to real estate, which the insured has an interest as owner, mortgagee or otherwise.

(a) Owner's Title Policy: Usually issued to the landowner himself. The owner's title insurance policy is bought and paid for only once, and then continues in force without any further payment. Owner's Title Insurance policies are not assignable.

(b) Mortgagee's Title Policy: Issued to the mortgagee and terminates when the mortgage debt is paid. In the event of foreclosure, or if the mortgagee acquires title from the mortgagor in lieu of foreclosure, the policy continues in force, giving continued protection against any defects of title which existed at, or prior to, the date of the policy.

Treasury Bills: Interest bearing U.S. Government obligations sold at a weekly sale. The change in interest rates paid on these obligations is frequently used as the Rate Index for Adjustable Mortgage Loans.

Truth in Lending (TIL): The name given to the federal statutes and regulations (Regulation Z) which are designed primarily to insure that prospective Borrowers of credit received credit and cost information before concluding a loan transaction.

Underwriting (Mortgage Loans): The process of evaluating a loan application to determine the risk involved for the lender. It involves an analysis of the borrower's creditworthiness and the quality of the property itself.

Verification of Deposit (VOD): Form used in mortgage lending to verify the deposits or assets of a prospective borrower when monthly statements are unavailable or unusable.

Verification of Employment (VOE): Form used in mortgage lending to verify the employment and income of a prospective borrower when pay stubs and W2 forms are unavailable or unusable.

Verification of Rent: Form used in mortgage lending to verify monthly rents paid and late payments, if any.

About Louis Brown

Investors have long regarded the training, systems and forms created by Louis "Lou" Brown as the best in the industry. Quoted as an expert by many publications such as *The Wall Street Journal* and *Smart Money,* Lou draws from his wide and varied background as a real estate investor. Having bought property since 1977, he has invested in single-family homes, apartments, hotels and developed subdivisions, as well as building and renovating homes and apartments. These experiences have given him a proving ground for the most cutting edge concepts in the real estate investment industry today. He is widely known as a creative financing genius regarding his deal structuring concepts. He enjoys sharing his discoveries with others as he teaches seminars and has authored courses, books and audio training on how to make money and keep it.

Lou is past President and a lifetime member of the Georgia Real Estate Investors Association and was founding President of the National Real Estate Investors Association. He firmly believes that the path to success is through ongoing education, and invests thousands of dollars annually in his own.

Lou loves to spend time in Atlanta with his beautiful wife Janice, their two children and foster daughter, and he always makes time to speak with other realtors and investors about his *Street Smart* and *Path to Homeownership* programs.

So if you are interested in learning how Lou can take you to the next level, then visit his website at **www.louisbrown.com** or contact him directly at **StreetSmartLouis@LouisBrown.com**.

Made in the USA
Columbia, SC
29 May 2024

36055796R00063